W9-BYK-511

THE LITTLE BOOK OF

THE LITTLE BOOK OF

Luxury

Add a touch of indulgence to your life

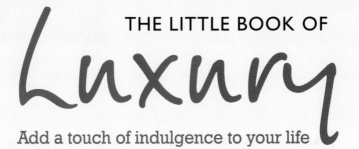

Nikki Page

CICO BOOKS
LONDON NEW YORK

For Sybil Kretzmer, an exceptional friend

Published in 2014 by CICO Books
An imprint of Ryland Peters & Small Ltd
20–21 Jockey's Fields,   519 Broadway, 5th Floor
London WC1R 4BW   New York, NY 10012

www.rylandpeters.com

10 9 8 7 6 5 4 3 2 1

Text © Nikki Page 2014
Design and photography © CICO Books 2014

The author's moral rights have been asserted. All rights reserved.
No part of this publication may be reproduced, stored in a retrieval system,
or transmitted in any form or by any means, electronic, mechanical, photocopying,
or otherwise, without the prior permission of the publisher.

A CIP catalog record for this book is available from the Library of Congress and the
British Library.

ISBN: 978 1 78249 116 3

Printed in China

Editor: Marion Paull
Designers: Geoff Borin and Isobel Gillan

For digital editions, visit www.cicobooks.com/apps.php

Contents

Introduction

*A little bit of luxury does you good
and makes you feel so much better.
But what is luxury?*

Luxury is doing or experiencing something you really enjoy. For those who are busy, the instant answer is often the time to indulge themselves with something special, be that a personal treat or spending uninterrupted time with friends or family. For those with too much time on their hands, the answer is more complex. It's finding something to do, someone to see, or bringing new experiences into their lives.

Of course, there are lots of easy answers to what is luxurious. In my own case, a spa treatment, time in the sunshine, or just having nothing to do come high on my list, but so do seeing bluebells and the first blossom of spring. Finding luxury every day is really about the way you approach life rather than spending lots of money.

UNDERSTANDING LUXURY

How pampered and happy you feel depends on your perspective on your own life. If you often feel envious of others or that life is somehow unkind to you, then it's harder to realize how many good things there are in your life. Admiring a person or noticing how much someone seems to have or how gifted someone is, watching from the outside, is very different from actually wanting to be in that person's shoes.

Take for example a gifted sportsman. He may have been born with natural talent but in order to be a national success, he will have to practice for hours and hours every single day. His whole life must revolve around his sport with little time for any sort of normal life, and the sure knowledge that his chosen career will end at a relatively young age. Think about those who are born very rich. Yes, they can shop till they drop and live in beautiful homes, but if that sort of luxury is the way to happiness, why do so many who have been given luxury on a plate experience drink or drug problems? The answer may be that what most of us think of as luxury has ceased to be pleasurable to them because the balance between earning and finding time and space for treasured experiences is lost. Then think of what may seem to be a perfect, long marriage or relationship. Talk more closely to the partners and discover how hard one or both may have worked to hold it together, and how many compromises each has made over the years. Being in a successful relationship is often just as much hard work as any career, particularly if you work and have children, too.

RECOGNIZING LUXURY

I am not suggesting that it is wrong to aspire to something that looks wonderful from the outside. Our aspirations are what define us, but be very honest about whether it is a life that you would actually choose. Look more closely at your own life and see all the things that others may admire in you. You are a very special person. Think of the people in your life—friends, family, neighbors, colleagues—the things you like best about yourself, a favorite physical feature, where you live, your work, your own talents, your solitude, and your spare time. How much do you really want to trade with someone else? How much better just to enhance the life you already have.

Luxury is as much about recognizing the good things in your life as it is about making the most of the time you have to enjoy something special. This book includes some tips on how to create spare time as well as ways to enjoy it. It aims to show that, regardless of whether you have time on your hands or are too busy, whether you are rich or distinctly feeling the pinch, there are many ways to bring luxury into your life.

SIMPLE LUXURY

Some of the most luxurious things in life are free but, for some reason, the very fact that they cost nothing, or very little, makes us take them for granted.

walking and nature

No matter where you live, spending time outdoors is one of the most luxurious things you can do.

Even in the most built-up areas, something wonderful will be growing somewhere, be it merely a beautiful wild flower living in a concrete crack. The fact is it's there and focusing on it stills the mind and relaxes the body.

Make sure that you plan time out of doors every day. Walk in a park and submerge yourself in the beauty of the different seasons. Take a close look at the amazing colors and textures that nature gives us. If you have a garden or yard, love and cherish it. Expensive plants are not necessary to make it beautiful. Wild cornflowers and poppies are stunning, as are bluebells, cow parsley, and rock plants. It doesn't matter where you live, something will grow naturally. If you have no garden or yard, do you have space for a pot or two, or a window box? You can even grow herbs or vegetables. There is little as delicious as something you've grown and nurtured yourself.

THE GREAT OUTDOORS

Just pottering around nature is wonderfully relaxing.

Listen to the birds, feed them in the winter, and help them to cope in an ever-
changing environment. You will be rewarded a thousand times over when you
watch and hear them. I have three pairs of different wild birds in my garden and
each spring is a delight as they welcome the start of the warmer weather. They
come really close when I'm pottering in my garden and seem to serenade me
with thank-yous for feeding them seeds and nuts through the cold months.

Whenever you can, walk to an appointment. Do try to vary your route a bit
to take in the different flowers and trees, hedgerows, and other people's
gardens. Walk through parks or take a prettier route, even if it's a little longer.
You'll arrive refreshed and happy, and will work and think better when you
get there. If you have to take public transport, use the time to look for beauty
from the windows. It's amazing how many shrubs grow in cities and how
many flower baskets are on display.

My favorite time of the year is spring—blossom and bluebells lift my spirits like
nothing else. Sometimes I just stand and stare at the blossom, losing myself in
myriad stunning florets and literally breathing in spring. It doesn't cost a cent
but it makes me happier than even a pair of Jimmy Choos could ever do!

laughter

As Charles Dickens said,

"There is nothing in the world so irresistibly contagious as laughter and good humour."

Forget everything else. If you're having a good belly laugh, giggling, or, even better, completely corpsed, you're really enjoying yourself. That's what luxury is—enjoying yourself! I have a dreadful laugh—it's rather dirty and definitely unladylike. I always remember a great girlfriend of mine, who is also a newspaper columnist, telling me I couldn't possibly succeed in politics if I didn't do something about my laugh! But that's one thing you cannot change about yourself, and neither should you. It's a piece of you that is entirely natural. I didn't continue in politics but I like to think that some people might have voted for me just because I knew how to laugh!

FIND HUMOR IN DAILY LIFE

Of course, you're more likely to laugh if you're with family or friends, but a good book or a favorite recording of something very funny works just as well if you're on your own. Victor Borge and Bob Newhart do it for me, as do some TV programs. Sometimes I find something I do myself positively hilarious when I am just going about my normal day. It can be a bit embarrassing when something strikes you as funny when you're riding along on the local bus, but I think most people find other people's laughter infectious and it brightens their day as well as yours.

sound

Wherever you are, you can create the luxury of your favorite sounds.

Ironically, that may mean starting with perfect stillness. If you sit quietly in a comfortable place, at home or out of doors, and just let everything go, you can cherish the sound of birds singing, waves pounding, the wind rustling through the trees, or the rain beating on the window.

You don't even have to be where the waves or the birds are. Plenty of recordings of nature's most beautiful sounds are available, and you can play them anywhere. You can be by a much-loved beach, in an English country garden, or in the depths of Africa or the jungles of the Amazon. You can play the sort of gentle, peaceful music that you hear in spas, or listen to the wind gently blowing through wind chimes.

Luxury can be noisy, too! Whether it's '60s rock & roll, pop, opera, beautiful voices, choirs, the most up-to-date chart-toppers, or the classics, enjoying the sound of music you love is uplifting and magical. Whether you sit in a comfortable chair with your feet up, lie on the bed, wallow in a perfect bath, or enjoy it while you're on the move, music is one of life's great luxuries.

warmth

Being warm automatically makes you feel good.

Snuggling up in bed with an extra blanket over the duvet in the winter and listening to the rain beating on the window is very nearly as luxurious as lying prone on a beach in glorious sunshine.

We identify being warm with feeling good. No matter the environment you're in, nothing is quite right if you're feeling a bit chilly. When my father passed away, I kept most of his sweaters, and when I'm at home feeling a bit on the cool side, I pop one on and instantly feel warm and cozy.

Curling up on a sofa with a warm blanket wrapped around you watching a movie is pretty good, too; as are lovely hot drinks of tea or chocolate, and a hot-water bottle in the bed on cold nights. Just making yourself warm and comfortable, wherever you are, sends an instant message to the brain that you are well and your life is luxurious.

But no matter how good it is to keep warm when the weather's cool, nothing is as wonderful as feeling warm sunshine on your face and body. That first really warm day of spring and the first time you can sit outside brightens the day as much as the longer, lighter evenings in the summer.

Simple Luxury 25

THE WARMTH OF KINDNESS

There are other ways of feeing warm, too. Warmth comes from the inside when you do something pleasant for someone else or when someone does something thoughtful for you. Kindness costs nothing to give or receive. When you look at another person's life and see a small way in which you can make it just a little better, make that very small effort. It is amazing how good you both feel and how kindness comes back to the giver. Help an old lady to carry her shopping or check on an elderly man who is home alone, lend your friend something to wear for a special date, or even just open doors for people following or preceding you. Kindness and politeness make your life, and everyone's life around you, better. Luxury indeed.

movement

*If you want to enjoy every day,
start each one with a few deep breaths
and some gentle yogic stretches.*

It is very difficult to feel good and enjoy life's pleasures if you can't breathe and move comfortably. In my previous book, *The Little Book of Wellbeing*, I start every section with the importance of breathing properly.

Of course, breath is life's great luxury. If we are not breathing, we are not here! But the quality of breath and the importance of keeping supple cannot be exaggerated.

Gemma McCoy, a young friend of mine, teaches yoga and breathing at Neal's Yard—a company who really cherish their personnel. They do everything they can to ensure that working with them, producing delicious creams and oils, is, in itself, a luxurious experience.

Here is one of Gemma's breathing exercises, recommended to de-stress, and a simple yogic stretch.

VILOMA
INTERRUPTED BREATH

This breathing technique allows your diaphragm full movement, which slows down your breathing, and is great to do if you're feeling anxious, having trouble sleeping, or experiencing menstrual tension.

✱ Lie down on your back, knees bent and arms by your side.

✱ Relax and breathe normally.

✱ Now add a pause to the inhale—so inhale 50 percent, pause for a moment, then inhale the other 50 percent, and exhale normally.

✱ If you find it easy, add another pause—so inhale one third, pause, inhale another third, pause, and then inhale the final third.

✱ If you find it difficult, you can do this on alternate breaths.

✳ We are not holding our breath—it's just a pause. Make each pause equal in length.

✳ Repeat for 10 cycles.

✳ Now, as you inhale, start moving your arms over your head to the floor behind you, holding your arms still each time you pause.

✳ Then bring your arms smoothly back to the floor beside you as you breathe out. Let the movement follow your breath, not the other way around.

✳ The more relaxed you are, the more the diaphragm can move, so don't over-extend your inhalation.

✳ Repeat all the above with the pause and arm movement on your exhalation. Note which one you prefer for your future practice.

✳ Be mindful of how you feel afterward.

ADHO MUKHA SVANASANA
DOWNWARD-FACING DOG

This pose is a great way to stretch our backs, and keeping the back flexible and spine straight is vital. A flexible and straight spine aids breathing and mobility, and may even help brainpower by ensuring oxygen is reaching every part of the brain. Also, luxury is not suffering back pain, as those who have it will testify!

✳ From an all-fours position with your wrists under your shoulders and knees under your hips, walk your hands one hand's length forward.

✳ Spread your fingers and press your palms and finger joints down on the mat.

✳ Tuck your toes under and take your hips as far back as you can toward your heels.

✳ Slowly start to push into your toes and lift your knees off the floor. The key is to keep taking your hips back without moving your hands. Imagine you have a long tail that someone is pulling!

✳ Straighten your legs, but only if you can keep a long spine. Very often, when students straighten their legs, the back rounds.

✳ Think of your energy shooting backward rather than rushing down through your arms. You should feel light in the arms.

✳ Keep your chin slightly tucked in, so the back of the neck is long.

✳ You can either stay there for 5 long breaths, or stay in motion, slowly lifting and lowering your knees.

✳ If you have a shoulder injury or find bending difficult, you can get the same effect by standing a yard (metre) or so away from the back of a chair or railing. Reach forward and place your hands over the back of the chair, spread your fingers, bend your knees a little, and draw your hips back to stretch the spine.

food

Food may be a necessity in life but that doesn't mean it shouldn't be a luxury, too.

We all have to eat, but many of us do not give enough thought to what we eat, how we eat it, and how to appreciate every mouthful. We eat too quickly, don't check the provenance of what we're eating, or, worst of all, waste precious food that is left over.

We should honor the food we eat and buy the best quality we can afford. We should be as sure as we can be that any animal involved has been respected before ending up on our plate. We should remember, too, how many people this planet is trying to feed, and respect the environment. Just being aware of what goes into your food already makes you appreciate it more.

My favorite restaurant in London is Brasserie Chavot. Eric Chavot is a highly acclaimed chef who has run double Michelin-starred restaurants for years. As soon as you arrive at Eric's eaterie, you sense the passion for food and for the environment that lies behind the door. The scent of fresh bay and lavender wafts across the front of the restaurant and a delightful display of old-fashioned garden roses sits inside the bay window.

The food is heaven-sent. Of course, most of us rarely eat at somewhere as special, so I asked Eric how he thought you could create such magic at home. He readily admitted that he sometimes ends up making dinner at home from a can of soup! But he doesn't do what most of us do, that is, open the can, pour it in to a saucepan, and heat it. Eric takes some garlic, chops it finely, and simmers it in a pan. Then he adds a few small pieces of dried or fresh chili, and when they are golden brown, in goes the soup, freshly ground salt, and cracked pepper. A splash of good olive oil and some fresh basil and parsley to garnish make a common or garden can of tomato soup taste fit for a king, and it takes just a very few minutes longer.

Eric insists, too, that whatever and whenever you eat, how you present the food makes a real difference to your experience and enjoyment of it. Be creative with your serving ware. Mix and match china to create a pleasing table or tray, and feast on how it looks even before the first bite!

Enjoy every mouthful and give gratitude to the animals and farmers who have given you your meal.

36 Simple Luxury

thankfulness

It doesn't matter how much you have or don't have, there is always something to be thankful for.

✳ If you live alone, be grateful for being able to do just as you please. You can eat what you like, when you like, and where you like, watch what you like on the TV, or listen to whatever music you choose. You can bathe when you like in an uncluttered bathroom!

✳ If you live in a hectic family environment or share with others, be glad for their companionship and the moments you share, for their love, and for the togetherness.

✳ If it is noisy where you are, treasure moments of peace.

✳ If you spend more time alone than you would like, be happy with the peace and find more ways to engage with others.

✳ If you are healthy, the world awaits you in a myriad of different ways. If you are not, think of ways to improve your health, and don't be a prisoner of your illness. Try not to be a victim of whatever has happened to you and make the most of your life, however long or short it is and in whatever way you can.

THE INSPIRATIONAL MATT KING

I work with Variety, the children's charity, and through that organization I met an amazing young man, Matt King. At 17 years old Matt was incredibly handsome, intelligent, and sporty. An extremely talented rugby player, he had been picked for his first Under-18 rugby tournament. He took a bad tackle and ended up paralyzed from the neck down, needing 24-hour care. He freely admits that he thought hard about asking to die, instead of which, after we had given him a fabulous motorized wheelchair, Matt went back to school, on to university, and qualified as a lawyer. He is the most awe-inspiring man I have ever met. He is still drop-dead gorgeous and with a character that makes him one of the most special people alive. For Matt, luxury is being able to go to watch England play rugby, and tilt his chair up so that he is "standing" like his friends while enjoying a beer through a straw. Matt finds so many things for which to give gratitude. For the rest of us, it gives taking a walk in the park a whole new meaning.

Give thanks for your experience of being here in this lifetime. You are here for a reason, whether you recognize it or not.

✳ If you have little money, be thankful for all the wonderful things that nature gives us for free. Make the most of what you have and don't waste it. Share what you do have with others in the knowledge that there are always people with less or in more difficulty.

✳ If you are financially secure, be grateful for all you have and be kind to others who have less, but be as grateful for those things that cost you nothing. Wealth on its own makes no one happy, although it certainly helps not to be broke!

✳ Give thanks for every friend, family member, and acquaintance who is in or passing through your life. Every one of them will teach you something you need to know.

✳ Count your blessings. I guarantee that you have way more than you think you have! When you feel a bit down, think of everything in your life that is good and for which you are genuinely thankful. Write them down, then bask in the luxury of living.

making time

*Now you've read this far you may be saying,
"But I don't have time for treats!" But you do!*

The first, and possibly the most important, step toward bringing luxury into your life every day is organizing your time. If your home is a mess, you can't find anything, you don't know what to wear, you don't know what you're going to eat in the evening, and nothing is ready for the day ahead, you're in such a frenzy by the time you leave the house that your journey to work, education, or vocation will be a nightmare as all the problems compete for attention in your stressed-out mind.

Imagine instead that you get out of bed in the morning with everything ready for breakfast, clothes ready to put on, and time for 10 minutes of yoga before you leave. It really isn't so difficult if you are organized.

Keep a little book in your bag, briefcase, or wherever you sit during the day, and by the bed at night, or use an electronic notebook on your phone. Never go anywhere without it! Decide on the categories on which you need to keep notes—children, home, shopping, work, and so on. Write down your priorities for today and later. Each night, check your list, cross off everything that's been done (very satisfactory), and update it for the following day.

Before going to bed, put water in the kettle or coffee machine, set out the breakfast things, and decide what you are going to wear.

Put children's sports kits ready by the door and take anything from the freezer you may need the next day. Going to bed with everything prepared and your list updated will help you to relax. If your mind isn't buzzing with concerns about what you have to do tomorrow, you will sleep better, which is already one of life's great luxuries.

Routine is a great maker of time. That is not to say that you shouldn't be flexible, but try to fix the basics in your life so that they are done at specific times, ensuring that you make space for those things you consider to be life's luxuries. I am an avid fan of fresh food and have my local farm producers deliver fresh vegetables and organic food to my door. They come every Tuesday and my order always goes in on Sunday night. I plan the meals around what needs eating up, so as not to waste, and shop in the supermarket for other essentials on Saturday or Sunday, meaning I don't have to worry about food for the rest of the week. I put older vegetables in a different drawer from newly bought ones so that I don't suddenly find something rotting under the fresh broccoli.

It's really a case of applying common sense to your life so you don't waste time chasing your own tail in a disorganized mess and missing out on the good stuff. Being organized also tends to save you money, leaving more for treats!

anticipating luxury

There is something extra special about anticipating luxury.

If you are not particularly well off, keep a separate bank account and, when you can, pay in, literally, a dollar, pound, or euro toward something just for you. When I was little, my family often struggled to make ends meet. My mother used to save whatever pennies she could in little, labeled pots in a drawer. It was amazing how the pennies added up and how much pleasure we had from having enough for a treat. That money was sacrosanct for whichever purpose was on the label. The fact that the treat had been saved for, and thought about, somehow made it even more exciting when the time came to spend the money. Nowadays, e-banking is the norm, and setting up one or two separate accounts to save small amounts is easy and safe.

Regular clearouts also help you to decide on things that have outlived their usefulness and that you can sell on the internet, at the local second-hand store, or at the auction house, but be sure to put the proceeds into a separate account to save for a luxury to enjoy. And if any item is not quite right to sell but could benefit someone else, donate it to your local thrift store or give it to someone who will appreciate it.

LUXURY IN THE HOME

First and foremost, keep your home neat.
It's much more difficult to relax and
enjoy a treat if everything around you is a
mess. When your home is neat, it helps to
calm the mind, too.

making your house a home

It may be that an Englishman's home is his castle, but more importantly, all our homes are our nests, where we are at our most private.

Home is where we cry, laugh, dream, awaken, and sleep, where we have our families and invite our closest friends. Castle or not, home is definitely where the heart is.

It's important to look at your home and see if it's really comfortable for you. Most of us can't afford to redecorate at will, or change the furniture whenever we feel like it. However, we can make plenty of small changes that may make a big difference to how we feel about our home.

In order to think about changes that may make you feel more comfortable and enjoy your home more, try to step back and see it afresh. Forget everything you're used to and think about rearranging. Could you move your pictures, or change the color of a wall here or there? Even moving the placement of a floormat can make a big difference.

Look at light. Are you blocking it anywhere, or making rooms unnecessarily dark? Open doors and windows whenever you can so your home is as light and airy as it can be.

I like to do up houses, and have moved often. In between homes, I usually rent for a few months while I work on my next project. Although I'm often in comparatively small spaces, I try to make my temporary home as cozy and comfortable as I would if it was permanent. I really enjoy fixing it up and turning it into my own little haven.

flowers

Fresh-cut flowers really do seem to change the
energy in the home. They somehow make any
apartment or house more welcoming.

Nowadays flowers are relatively inexpensive to buy from supermarkets
or flower stalls, and you don't need many to make a big difference.
If you are lucky enough to have a garden or yard, add some greenery
to the bought flowers to make them look as if they came from your own
garden or from a florist's store.

In spring, flowers remind us that winter is over; in summer, their beautiful scents can waft through our home; in fall, their rich colors brighten up the darker evenings; and in winter, we can add Christmas decoration or splashes of color to warm our days and lift our spirits.

Flowers are magical. The delicacy of their florets, colors, and scents is quite wonderful, and just a little time spent studying a flower and allowing our senses to take in its natural beauty can transform our mood and bring light into our lives. Flowers are an inexpensive luxury but one that is hard to beat.

organizing your wardrobe

Keep your closets neat!

My niece thinks I'm positively obsessive because I keep all my white tops in one place, black in a different pile, and so on. Skirts, pants, and jackets are hung by color, so when I'm deciding what to wear, I can easily mix and match the right outfit for the occasion. Navy and black are never hung or stored together, so I don't suddenly find I'm wearing odd-colored socks! Similarly, shoes are all stored in boxes or pouches by color, so they're easy to find and stay looking good. Nothing is put away creased or dirty.

Look after your clothes and keep them looking good. If you can, change into something easy and comfortable the minute you step through the door, and hang up your work or daytime clothes right away. If they're dirty, put them straight in the laundry basket, or to one side ready to take to the cleaners.

Organize your accessories. A cutlery tray works very well for costume jewelry—bracelets in one compartment, rings in another, and so on—or you can buy small plastic boxes with drawers, which keep those necklaces and earrings dust-free as well as organized, making it easy to find the right accessories for a chosen outfit.

Keep out the moths. Wrap color-sorted knitwear in moth-proof or polythene bags, or vacuum pack and keep clothes in hanging bags wherever possible. It's really upsetting to lose a favorite sweater to hungry, inconsiderate moths! If you separate your clothes into different parcels, at least if the moth gets one, it won't get into them all.

If you take care of your things and use your imagination, you'll be amazed at how long they last. This means more savings for other luxuries.

I love taking a jacket that is slightly dated and changing the shoulders or sleeves, or adjusting the cut, so that it feels almost new to wear. Sometimes just adding a belt or different accessories really changes the look of an old favorite. Splitting up suits and wearing the bottoms or tops with alternatives is a great way of increasing the scope of your wardrobe. There's something immensely satisfying about discovering different outfits in your existing collection of clothes.

Finding sartorial luxury with friends

If you have a couple of close friends who are about the same size, a fun thing to do is to go through each other's closets. I'll almost guarantee you that you'll look quite different in any given dress or pair of pants. You'll try colors you never thought you could wear and love the look. You'll accessorize differently and see things in one another's outfits that you haven't noticed in your own. Find the things that work best on each other, be creative in suggesting a change in the shoulder line here or a tuck there, and, above all, swap clothes.

Most of us are quite clear in our minds about what we think suits us. Good friends not only add insight to your wardrobe but also buy different types of clothes themselves. We all make mistakes in our purchases. What better than to give a "mistake" to a good friend and see her look wonderful in it, rather than let it grow stale at the back of your closet? And how perfect to receive a new outfit that is very different from everything else you have and didn't cost a penny. It is great fun and an all-round win.

Luxury is never feeling stressed about what you're going to wear, feeling confident in your choice of apparel, and never finding that your favorite outfit has a stain on the front or a hole in the sleeve!

luxurious bed

One of the most wonderful treats is fresh bed linen and a beautifully made bed.

Going to a multiple-star hotel and seeing that exquisite bed, artistically laid out, and climbing between beautiful, freshly scented sheets, has to be one of life's great luxuries.

In one of London's most famous hotels, the Savoy, they take every single detail of the room very seriously indeed. For more than a century, the Savoy has been a second home to some of the world's most famous people, and nothing is left to chance. While the newest ideas are incorporated into every area of the hotel, tradition is cherished to ensure the most luxurious stay possible.

The finest cotton is used to make the sheets, which are sprayed with lavender or rose water during ironing, so that the soft scent promotes uninterrupted sleep for the weary traveller. Beds are made with artistic flair and then turned down before night falls, ensuring beautiful counterpanes are not creased overnight and the bed looks so tempting that you can't wait to climb in.

Few of us have the wherewithal to create quite such a spectacular bedroom in our own home, but there are things we can do for a special treat:

✳ Why not buy some rose or lavender water and spray your sheets with it when you are ironing them, or if they're of the non-iron variety, spray them when they're drying for that lovely fresh scent when you go to bed.

✳ Treat yourself to a professional laundry service now and again so that the sheets and pillowcases are beautifully ironed.

✳ Work at making your bed look lovely in your bedroom, with extra pillows and throws.

✳ Turn your counterpane down an hour or so before you retire for the night, so that your bed looks particularly welcoming when the time comes.

✳ Make bedtime a ritual that relaxes you before you go to sleep. A scented candle by the bed (be very sure to blow it out before switching off the light) and a spot of sleep-inducing aromatherapy oil on the wrists and on your chest create a lovely relaxing atmosphere for uninterrupted sleep. All sorts of mixes of aromatherapy oil are available—just find one you love.

china and glass

Luxury makes you feel special.

How you lay a table or set a breakfast or tea tray turns something mundane into something far more enjoyable. It really doesn't take any longer to make something look lovely than it does just to throw it all together. In addition, the more care you put into the preparation, the more you're likely to enjoy the experience.

This tip is for those who live either on their own or with one other person. If you have a family, it is something you can enjoy when everyone else is out!

Prepare your breakfast tray the night before, using pretty china and attractive cutlery. Add a tea or coffee cozy to keep your drink hot, and pop a single flower on the tray. I put everything ready, including my cereal in the bowl, cover it, put water in the kettle, and then all I have to do in the morning is heat the water, pour milk into the pitcher, and take my breakfast back to bed with my newspaper. I prop the pillows up in my bed and enjoy every second. For me, this is the height of indulgence and luxury, and a wonderful way to start the day. As an alternative, in the summer, I take my tray into the garden and enjoy my breakfast in the early morning sun.

If I am entertaining friends, how the table looks is as important as every other part of the occasion. I love to set it using my best things, varying the look depending on how I am feeling. Sometimes I spread a pretty cloth that I inherited from my grandmother, and set the table with old-fashioned china and traditional glassware. Other times, the setting is sleek and modern. I always have proper napkins and candles on the table. I make sure the glassware is shining and the cutlery freshly polished. Napkins are folded into the glasses to make the table look inviting—somehow, it does make the food taste better!

For tea in the afternoon, how luxurious to set it out on a tray with a freshly laundered tray cloth, lovely china, and something moderately wicked on a matching plate! Sit, preferably with your feet up, and enjoy a few minutes off, or read something you need to read while you're relaxed and happy.

It is amazing how you can do these things quite quickly but how they bring a real feeling of luxury into your life.

scents, candles, and aromatic oils

There are so many beautifully scented candles around that it is now easy to turn your home into a relaxing haven.

In the evening, as soon as I sit down to eat, read, listen to music, or even watch television, I light my candles in the room I'm in, or burn some aromatic oil.

Aromatic oils are readily available and they last for ages in a burner, particularly if you buy the waxy ones that melt. I have a cabinet full of votives, which heat the oil or look great in a variety of different containers on their own. But you can create your own scents by mixing aromatherapy oils to suit your mood. Ylang ylang, jasmine, or peony are beautifully uplifting, while rosemary will refresh you and lavender will calm you down.

CANDLES

Candles instantly transform a room from mere living space to a place of tranquility. It is not just the aroma that does it, but also the soft light that reflects around the room once the candles are lit.

I have candles in my sitting room, my bedroom, and my bathroom. In the evening, they are lit wherever I am. Subconsciously, candles help me to relax and finish my day so that I'm more likely to have a good night's sleep and awake feeling ready for the following day.

Candles create a romantic as well as a relaxing environment. Who doesn't want candles on the table for that special dinner? But whether sharing or alone, they make you feel cozy and loved.

Candles are a fabulous gift to give and receive. A gift of a scented candle carries a silent message—relax and pamper yourself.

bathroom spa

If a visit to a spa isn't on the agenda, you can create a wonderful spa at home.

Bath time should be a time of unadulterated luxury. Normally, the easiest way to make the best of bath time is to take your bath before going to bed. How you dress your bathroom, what you put in your bath, and what you do afterward all go towards making this a daily treat.

Unwinding at the end of the day is important for your health and vitality. If you de-stress and let go of the day's irritation before climbing between those lavender-scented sheets, you will sleep very much better and awake refreshed.

Firstly, clear the bathroom of any clutter that shouldn't be there. You can't relax in a mess. Make sure you have clean, preferably warm, fluffy towels to hand. Then create the atmosphere of a luxurious spa—play some relaxing music, and light scented candles or votives displayed in pretty holders. Run a hot bath and pour in some of your favorite oil under the tap so the scent permeates your bathroom. It can be a purchased bath oil, or add a few drops of your chosen aromatherapy oil to a little almond oil to create your own bath-time treat. Try not to use bubble baths if you have dry skin because they will only dry it out even more, and they often contain chemicals.

Cath Collins creates gorgeous bath oils and I particularly love her Lilyfandango in my bath. It combines lilies and jasmine with a hint of patchouli and cedar. Delicious! But I also mix lavender and ylang ylang for relaxation and a deep night's sleep after a hectic day. I experiment all the time with different oils and find that my choices change with my mood and the time of day I take my bath. It is important to give yourself permission to relax. So often, we don't think we have time or deserve to relax and enjoy something that is just for us, but we do!

When you have had your bath, wrap yourself in your warm towel and then rub a scented cream all over your body. Try to use an organic product. Remember, whatever you put on your skin is absorbed into your body, and you don't want non-organic substances rushing around your system. Find local organic companies and support them. You'll find that knowing you're being kind to your skin and the environment makes you feel even more relaxed.

If you don't have time for a long bath but need to relax before going to bed, try this suggestion for a hand massage from Cath Collins:

Take a little almond oil and mix it with a few drops of an essential oil that fits your mood. This makes a delicious, soothing treat for your hands. Pour a little into the palm of your hand and smooth into the skin on the back of your other hand; work up each finger individually and massage the cuticles. Do that for each hand. Go back to the palms of your hands, massage each in turn with a thumb, not forgetting the base of your fingers, and then stroke up and over your wrists. It's great to do this just before you turn out the light so that your hands benefit from the oil overnight.

chocolate

Surely one of the universe's greatest gifts!

Although I have a sensitive stomach, I find real chocolate does me nothing but good—so much good that I have it every day! It is truly one of my favorite treats.

Chocolate is one luxury that must be of very good quality. Cheap chocolate is full of sugar, preservatives, and additives, and is not good for you at all. However, organic, high cocoa-content chocolate has been shown to be good for the heart, and it's certainly one of the best comforters you can have. There is nothing like sitting down with a cup of tea and a piece of chocolate, to read or watch a movie or TV. Somehow chocolate just makes life better!

A great deal of chocolate is usually at least six weeks old. One way to avoid this is to order online so that it comes to you direct from the maker. At My Swiss Chocolate, not only do they send your chocolates straight from the kitchen, but also you can choose your own flavors and invent your own recipes. They come beautifully decorated and packaged. The bars have flowers embedded in them, which makes them look very special and lifts your spirits even before you take a bite. You can also send a "chocolate postcard" to a friend. My own preferences include Rose, Jasmine Tea, and Caramel and Salt. They list recipes online, so you can try other chocolate-lovers' particular favorites.

HOT CHOCOLATE

Another fabulous way to enjoy chocolate is, of course, to drink it hot.

There is probably no better hot chocolate in the world than that produced by the exquisite chocolatiers, Rococo. Their 70 percent hot chocolate is rich and intense, containing only organic dark chocolate, flaked and mixed with a little extra cocoa powder.

The best way to make hot drinking chocolate is to pour a very small amount of very hot water onto the drinking chocolate in a mug to create a smooth paste. Then choose how you want to drink your chocolate:

✳ ESPRESSO: Add a small amount of hot water to give you an intense, thick shot of chocolate.

✳ LONG: Fill your mug with hot water or milk (coconut, almond, or soya if you don't take dairy,) depending on how dark or milky you like your chocolate. Don't add sugar—it will spoil that lovely rich, pure chocolate.

✳ INDULGENT: Top up with warm cream and stir well. For a really thick hot chocolate, heat until the cream boils briefly and the hot chocolate thickens.

Once you've made your hot chocolate you can try adding different flavors by dropping in a twist of orange peel or using a cinnamon stick as a stirrer.

an afternoon off watching your favorite sport

Yes, I know it's very bad to be a couch potato and not get the exercise you need. Indeed, exercise can be a luxury in itself. However, there is something wonderfully sinful and luxurious about settling in for an afternoon of watching your favorite sport.

I love Formula 1 motor racing, rugby, and tennis from Wimbledon. I live on my own, so picking what I want to watch is easy, but if you share your life with others, you can easily share your favorite sports and take turns in selecting what to watch.

Make sure that you really prepare for your afternoon off. Have all the chores done in time for the start of your program and set a tray with some treats. Fill the kettle so you can jump up in the pauses or when things are either too nerve-wracking or in a lull to make a quick cup of tea or coffee.

Your treat tray is important. As a healthy eater, my snacks are always good for me. I promise that doesn't take away in the slightest from thoroughly enjoying my feet-up time.

DECADENT LUXURY

When traveling, I like to try different spas and experience local customs and treatments. Even when I'm pampering myself at home, I make an effort to try unusual or new types of beauty therapy.

coconut hair treatment

The most luxurious hair treatment I ever experienced was in a super-luxury hotel in the Seychelles, where the treatments are inspired by ancient Indian and Asian traditions.

After I had chilled out in the glorious relaxation lounge overlooking the ocean, the therapist took me to a pavilion where I lay down listening to sounds of the ocean.

The therapist gently parted my hair and massaged in copious amounts of locally produced coconut oil, until my hair was drenched from roots to tips. As the oil did its work, I was treated to a beautiful head and foot massage. The longer the oil is left on, the better the result, and so, since I was leaving the following morning, I scraped my hair back into a neat chignon and left the oil in until I reached home. Once clean, my hair felt amazing. It was soft and glossy, and the memory of all that pampering helped to keep me relaxed all the way home.

If you don't have the time or the budget to hop on a plane to the glorious Seychelles, you can achieve much the same results at home.

DECADENCE ON A BUDGET

Set aside an evening to treat yourself to some time out. Pop into your local pharmacy and buy yourself a hair-coloring brush, and into the health store for a pot of organic coconut oil. You will need about two tablespoons of the oil, so you will have plenty left for more treatments or cooking. Make your preparations—ensure your bathroom is neat, have fresh towels at the ready, light some candles, play some sea sounds or your favorite relaxing music, and run a warm, scented bath.

Have your coconut oil ready, and your coloring brush, a wide-toothed comb, and a shower cap. Using the stem of the coloring brush, part the hair in sections and brush the oil down each parting as if you were going to color it. Comb the oil all the way through your hair, ensuring that it soaks in to the tips. Gently massage your scalp and then put on the shower cap. Now climb into that hot bath and relax for as long as you like, letting the steam increase the effect of the oil on your hair.

Afterward, take to your bed and chill. In the morning, wash the oil out of your hair thoroughly and dry as normal. Your hair will look great and you will feel pampered—even if you don't have a suntan!

South African spa

I am lucky to have family in Cape Town, and so I get to visit now and again. On a recent trip, I visited two wonderful but very different spas.

The first was an oasis of serenity, whose central philosophy is "Unwind, Restore, and Elevate." So much about understanding luxury is knowing the importance of de-stressing and making time for yourself wherever you are. At the spa, they assess each person and suggest treatments to help restore their inner calm and energy levels.

One time when I went to the spa, I had left a very wet and cold English winter to visit my niece in beautifully sunny Cape Town, but I had experienced a nasty bug and had flown in cramped conditions for 12 hours. It's very unusual for me to feel bad and I'm happy to say that, applying my own remedies (_The Little Book of Wellbeing_,) I was quickly on the road to recovery. However, my back still ached and my shoulders, always my particular bugbear, were solid as the rock I was standing on.

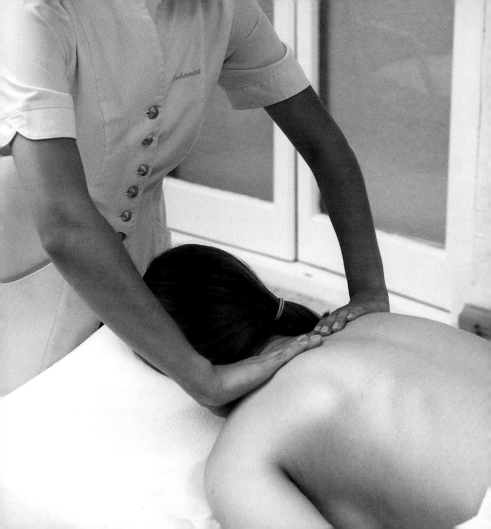

To ease the aches, I had a lovely steam followed by a Jacuzzi bath, taking advantage of the differently shaped, extra-pressure water jets to start the work on my tired muscles.

Rosie, my personal advisor, suggested I try the Essence of Africa Journey. This is a 60-minute back massage, using age-old healing ingredients, such as baobab tree oil and rooibos herbs from the African bush. These uplift the senses, improve skin elasticity, and reduce stress. Even more exciting for those of us who have never experienced such a thing before, the therapist employs a wooden rungu stick to ensure that not a single knot or spot of tension is left anywhere in your whole back. I loved it! Lying in the beautiful natural surroundings, warmed by the South African summer sun, being perfectly de-stressed was quite simply blissful.

Of course, popping into a spa like this isn't regularly possible for most of us. Rosie's tip for de-stressing at home is to pop a few drops of any herbal essence that you may have, or a spoonful of loose tea leaves, in the bath under the running hot water. Let them disperse and allow the aroma to seep into your senses. Soak your tired and stressed body for at least 10 minutes for maximum benefit to the skin and senses.

Consider adding green tea to your bath for a natural detox; cranberry and raspberry to help revitalize you; lemon to uplift you; lavender and ylang ylang to help you to relax.

enjoying luxury together

My second South African experience was very different! It was still wonderfully pampering but also somewhere designed to enjoy treats with friends.

Set in the Wineries about 30 miles out of Cape Town, with stunning views all around, the spa seeks to empower women from disadvantaged and underprivileged backgrounds to harness their innate healing abilities. The spa is intended as an African sanctuary, bringing together a variety of massage therapies and centuries-old African healing rituals.

This spa also encourages newcomers to spas to experience their retreat without the normal rigors of spa discipline. For a start, there is a bar and copious amounts of cake!

My niece and I joined one of their Africa Day Revitalize Packages. For my niece, this meant a day away from caring for two young children and working in between. Our welcome could not have been warmer, and it was immediately apparent that everyone there really wants you to enjoy every moment and that this day is for sharing.

At the start of the day, everyone assembles in the main area for a light breakfast and a traditional African welcome of drumming and singing. You then have a choice of treatments that range from neo matsogo, a royal African hand massage, to thiapiso, a full-body-cleansing spa ritual. When you have hand or foot massages, you all sit side by side in comfortable chairs, looking across the beautiful countryside.

Between treatments, you return to the main area for light refreshment. In the middle of the day, a delicious lunch is provided, and more entertainment, and, of course, the option of a glass of wine or a large piece of chocolate cake. Don't go here for slimming!

What was so special about this day was that my niece and I were able to enjoy all of it together, and the breaks with the wonderful local entertainment were delightful.

This is the only spa of its kind that I have visited but it reminded me that taking proper time out with someone you really care about is a true luxury. Choose something you both thoroughly enjoy but might not do on your own, or perhaps something that you feel just a little bit guilty about! Give one another permission to revel in the time together and the time away from all the daily stresses. Enjoy every second of it. When you return to life as normal, you'll be refreshed and have more energy and love for all those who rely on you, and all the things you need to do.

the joy of facials

Having a facial is one of life's luxuries that should really be considered an essential!

Your face and skin are among the first things that people notice—they are what you wear in public every day. A good-quality monthly facial works wonders to improve the skin's texture, keeping lines at bay and promoting a healthy, toned, and radiant complexion. One of my favorite treatments is a facial that I have at the Renaissance St Pancras Spa in London. It incorporates ancient Japanese massage techniques that give a manual facelift. The extensive massage is super-relaxing and makes your skin look and feel better.

When choosing facials, I always think it's important to select somewhere that uses natural products. Once of my favorite brands is Cinq Mondes, which uses beauty secrets and recipes dating back to ancient Egyptian times.

For regularly looking after your own complexion, expert Rachel Lowe suggests:

Exfoliate once a week!

This makes a big difference to your skin and makes all your other skincare products more effective as they are able to penetrate deeper and work on your healthy skin cells. Remember to choose something natural and gentle. The reason most people give for not exfoliating their skin regularly is that they don't have time, but there is no excuse as it need take no longer than a few minutes that can be easily incorporated into your daily routine. I personally use a product that exfoliates and nourishes at the same time. I apply it just before I get into the shower so the steam helps it do its work and I can wash it off during my shower. It takes no extra time at all! I prefer this to a regular scrub as it is much less harsh on the skin. Some scrubs can be too abrasive and scratch the skin's surface. A good mask or exfoliator will naturally and gently break down the dead skin cells. Whatever else you do, you must cleanse, tone, and moisturize every day.

Sarah Strang from Cinq Mondes gave me advice and a special massage to do at home, allowing me to enjoy a little bit of pampering even during my daily routine. She said:

Be sure to clean your face morning and evening every day, but make giving it a special cleanse with a deep cleanser a real treat. This quick massage can be done at home and works wonders at boosting the blood circulation, leaving skin plump and brimming with a healthy glow. Use your forefinger and middle finger to gently massage in circular motions, working from the center of the chin up towards the ear, then use the same motion from mouth to ear, and nose to ear, working gently upward before reaching the eye contour where you should then use the middle finger to dab lightly from the inner eye contour out towards the ear—this will also help to reduce puffiness. Then, on the forehead, start in the center and again work outward, massaging to smooth the skin and cleansing as you go. I love to use a hot face cloth to remove my cleanser afterwards. It only takes about five minutes and I try to do this twice a week. It's my little luxury and a moment for myself where I instantly look and feel better.

conclusion

TIPS FOR FINDING LUXURY IN LIFE

Two of the key points that bring about <u>unhappiness in life are judgment</u> <u>and expectation.</u>

Too many of us are disappointed in others because they don't act in the way we want them to, instead of accepting people for themselves. That doesn't mean that either you or they are wrong; we are all as we are meant to be. We can benefit from what we learn in good relationships with others as they can from being with us, but we are inevitably different <u>and we should honor the differences as much as we enjoy the similarities.</u> If the differences are too great, we do not have to spend much time with them, but we should not judge them. Therein lies the way to anger, bitterness, and sleepless nights.

Similarly, expectation can be a very dangerous thing. If you are sure that you deserve promotion and then someone else is more successful than you, the disappointment of expectation can leave you seriously upset. But if you accept that it wasn't your job, you can move easily to re-evaluating your position and deciding what you want to do. If you are looking forward to a weekend off being a certain way, or the person you're sharing it with behaving in a certain way, you may, just by that thought, limit how much you are going to enjoy yourself.

Enjoying a truly luxurious life is much more about your approach to life than the amount of money you can spend. I'd like to think that this Little Book has given you some inspiration and that by reading it you have found ways to enhance your life, or perhaps it has highlighted areas that you will now find more fulfilling. I hope so.

MY ADDRESS BOOK

Eric Chavot: www.brasseriechavot.com

Cath Collins fragrances: www.cathcollins.com

Cinq Mondes beauty products: www.cinqmondes.com

Four Seasons Hotel, Seychelles: www.fourseasons.com/seychelles/spa

Mangwanani: www.mangwanani.co.za

Gemma McCoy, yoga instructor: www.gemmamccoy.com

My Swiss Chocolate: www.myswisschocolate.ch

Neal's Yard Remedies: www.nealsyardremedies.com

One & Only Spa, Cape Town: spa.reservations@oneandonlycapetown.com

Renaissance St Pancras Spa: www.stpancrasspa.co.uk

Rococo Chocolates: www.rococochocolates.com

Tea Palace: www.teapalace.com

The Savoy Hotel, London: www.fairmont.com/savoy

Variety, the children's charity: www.variety.org.uk

Welsh Lavender Ltd: www.welshlavender.com

INDEX

ACKNOWLEDGMENTS

To those who bring luxury into my life and inspired this book:

Anne and Adrian, who helped me to find the luxury of my own spiritual path.

Hazel, who introduced me to my publisher and has brought so much luxury into my life through knowledge, guidance, and a great deal more.

My stunning friends: Anne-Marie, Caroline, Chris, Cristina, Jenifer, Jennie, Liz, Louise, Mandy, Pamela, Patience, Rowan, Vivienne, who bring me the luxuries of companionship, fabulous friendship, laughter, and wisdom.

John, who is always so supportive and the best friend anyone could have.

My brother and sister-in-law, Stuart and Jenny, who have given me the luxury of fabulous family get-togethers, two wonderful nieces and a seriously cool nephew.

To those nieces and nephew, Sarah, Rebecca, and Patrick, their partners and combined six offspring, who bring the luxury of family life to me and a great deal of joy.

Cindy, Lauren, and Penny at Cico, who make writing and publishing a truly delightful experience.

Picture Credits:

© Debi Treloar: 1, 7, 37, 44, 55, 70; David Montgomery: 2, 66, 73, 86, 87; Dan Duchars: 3, 93; Kate Whitaker: 5, 89; James Merrell: 9; Winfried Heinze: 10, 90; Polly Wreford: 12, 13, 39, 59, 60, 63, 101, 105, 109; Peter Cassidy: 15, 98; Tim Platt /cultura/ Corbis: 18; Pete Leonard / Corbis: 20; Melanie Eclare: 23; Chris Tubbs: 24; Christopher Drake: 27, 40; Emma Mitchell: 29; Geoff Dann: 32; Mark Lohman: 35, 53; Simon Brown: 43; Kate Kunz / Corbis: 47; Mark Scott: 48, 49, 52, 65; Jan Baldwin: 51, 75; Simon Brown: 56; Catherine Gratwicke: 57; Sandra Lane: 58; Claire Richardson: 97; Diana Miller: 69; Chris Everard: 77, 85, 95; Lucinda Symons: 78; Richard Jung: 81, 82; Carolyn Barber: 106.